WITHDRAWN

Jesse Owens

Jesse Owens

BY MERVYN KAUFMAN

Illustrated by Larry Johnson

Thomas Y. Crowell Company   New York

CROWELL BIOGRAPHIES
Edited by Susan Bartlett Weber

JANE ADDAMS *by Gail Faithfull Keller*
MARIAN ANDERSON *by Tobi Tobias*
LEONARD BERNSTEIN *by Molly Cone*
MARTHA BERRY *by Mary Kay Phelan*
WILT CHAMBERLAIN *by Kenneth Rudeen*
RAY CHARLES *by Sharon Bell Mathis*
CESAR CHAVEZ *by Ruth Franchere*
SAMUEL CLEMENS
by Charles Michael Daugherty
ROBERTO CLEMENTE *by Kenneth Rudeen*
CHARLES DREW *by Roland Bertol*
FANNIE LOU HAMER *by June Jordan*
LANGSTON HUGHES, AMERICAN POET
by Alice Walker
JAMES WELDON JOHNSON
by Ophelia Settle Egypt

FIORELLO LA GUARDIA
by Mervyn Kaufman
THE MAYO BROTHERS *by Jane Goodsell*
JOHN MUIR *by Charles P. Graves*
JESSE OWENS *by Mervyn Kaufman*
GORDON PARKS *by Midge Turk*
ROSA PARKS *by Eloise Greenfield*
THE RINGLING BROTHERS *by Molly Cone*
JACKIE ROBINSON *by Kenneth Rudeen*
ELEANOR ROOSEVELT *by Jane Goodsell*
MARIA TALLCHIEF *by Tobi Tobias*
JIM THORPE *by Thomas Fall*
THE WRIGHT BROTHERS
by Ruth Franchere
MALCOLM X *by Arnold Adoff*

Copyright © 1973 by Mervyn Kaufman. Illustrations copyright © 1973 by Larry Johnson. All rights reserved. Except for use in a review, the reproduction or utilization of this work in any form or by any electronic, mechanical, or other means, now known or hereafter invented, including xerography, photocopying, and recording, and in any information storage and retrieval system is forbidden without the written permission of the publisher. Published simultaneously in Canada by Fitzhenry & Whiteside Limited, Toronto.

Manufactured in the United States of America   ISBN 0-690-45934-3   0-690-45935-1 (LB)

3 4 5 6 7 8 9 10

Library of Congress Cataloging in Publication Data Kaufman, Mervyn D. Jesse Owens. SUMMARY: An easy-to-read biography of the black athlete who won four gold medals in the 1936 Olympics. 1. Owens, Jesse, 1913- 1980 Juv. lit. [1. Owens, Jesse, 1913- 1980 2. Athletes. 3. Negroes—Biography.] I. Johnson, Larry, illus. GV697.O9K38 796.4'2'0924 [B] [92] 72-83787 ISBN 0-690-45934-3 ISBN 0-690-45935-1 (lib. bdg.)

Jesse Owens

Jesse Owens was once the fastest man in the world. He could run faster and jump farther than anyone. But when he was little, he was sickly and weak. His parents were afraid he would die.

He was born near Oakville, Alabama, on September 12, 1913. His father, Henry Owens, worked for a rich man who owned a cotton farm. Like other poor blacks, Mr. Owens often worked in the fields from four-thirty in the morning until eight at night. Even so, he barely earned enough money to buy food for the family and pay rent for his little house.

Mr. Owens and his wife, Emma, had seven children. There were four sons and three daughters.

Jesse's three older brothers helped their father in the fields after school. But Jesse was too frail to work. Every winter he got sick. His mother nursed him back to health with loving care and homemade medicines.

One winter when Jesse was sick, he nearly died of cold. There wasn't enough wood to keep the fireplace going, and he couldn't get warm. The Owens house was made of thin boards that always let the cold in.

Mrs. Owens wanted the family to move north. She had heard that people were not so poor there. But her husband was afraid to leave the South. He couldn't read or write. What would he do in the North, he wondered.

He and Emma talked about it a lot. Finally, in

1921, they decided to go. Henry Owens sold all his tools and his five mules. He moved the family to Cleveland, Ohio.

Life was no better for them there, because work was hard to find. Mr. Owens rarely had a steady job. Sometimes he washed windows. Sometimes he swept floors. Mrs. Owens worked as a cleaning lady.

The family ate beans and onions, potatoes and onions, or bread and onions. There was never enough food to go around and almost never any meat. Often they came close to starving.

Still, though he looked frail, Jesse Owens grew stronger and taller. By the time he was twelve, he could beat any of his friends whenever they ran races at school.

One day, after winning a race, Jesse met Charles Riley, coach of the track team at the junior high school. Mr. Riley trained boys on the team to run fast and jump high and far.

Coach Riley was surprised that a boy so skinny could run so well. He thought that by running a little each day, Jesse might be able to go even faster. And perhaps, someday, he could get on the track team.

Jesse said he didn't have time to run. He had to work after school to earn money. All the Owens children had jobs. "Why don't you run before school?" said the coach. Jesse agreed.

He met Riley on the sidewalk outside the school every morning. Jesse ran for forty-five minutes, until the bell rang. Mr. Riley coached him, helping him run faster and farther. Mr. Riley helped him in other ways. Sometimes he brought Jesse food.

"See how this tastes," he would say. "My wife cooked it." He could see that Jesse didn't get much to eat at home.

Coach Riley was the first white man Jesse ever knew, and Jesse came to love him very much.

Time passed, but Jesse's legs still looked as thin as sticks beside the other boys'. "I won't be good enough to get on the team this year," he said sadly.

"Who says you have to make it this year?" said Riley, smiling. "You're training for four years from next Friday."

Mr. Riley kept saying this, "four years from next Friday," week after week and month after month for two years.

Finally Jesse did get on the track team. And one day he set a record. He ran a hundred yards in only ten seconds.

He also worked very hard at night and after school. He pumped gas in a filling station. He ran an elevator. Often he had as many as three jobs at once.

In 1931, when he was eighteen, he married Ruth Solomon. They were both in high school and had been sweethearts since grammar school. Their first home was a tiny two-room apartment.

Hardly anybody noticed Jesse in high school, until he entered a big track meet along with athletes from all over the country. He won the 100-yard dash, the 200-yard dash, and the broad jump.

Now a lot of people knew who he was. Newspaper reporters wrote stories about him. Colleges sent people to see him.

Each college wanted him on its track team. Four years of college would cost a lot of money, but the schools were willing to pay it all.

Just then Jesse's father lost the job he had. It had paid only twelve dollars a week, but now he was earning nothing. The family scraped by on what money Emma and the children brought in.

Jesse said no to all the colleges. He couldn't live like a rich man while his father struggled to find work. He even quit the track team.

But he was very sad. For days he talked to no one, not even to his wife, Ruth.

Then Charles Riley came to see him. Mr. Riley was still his coach and his friend.

"If I could get your father a steady job, would you go to college?" he asked.

"There are no steady jobs for Negroes," Jesse told him.

"But if there were," said Riley, "would you join the team again?"

Jesse thought a moment. "Yes," he replied.

So Riley made a trip to Ohio State University. There he spoke about Jesse with Larry Snyder, the best track coach in the country.

Snyder knew that many colleges had tried to get Jesse to come. "We don't have as much money as they do," he said.

"He doesn't want money," Riley explained. "He wants to work. And he wants his father to have a job, too."

When Riley returned to Cleveland, he had two

letters for Jesse. One said that Ohio State University wanted him as a student. Three jobs were waiting for him, so he could pay his own way.

The other letter said that his father would have a job with the state of Ohio for as long as he wished. Jesse was so happy he threw his arms around Riley and kissed him.

Ruth stayed in Cleveland when Jesse went off to college in Columbus, Ohio. He worked hard, studied until late at night, and trained with the track team every day.

The team had only a few Negroes. They lived in the same house and ate all their meals together.

Whenever there was a track meet at another school, they traveled in the same car.

One morning Jesse and three black teammates were on their way to a meet in Indiana. They had been driving since dawn. The white members of the team rode in cars ahead of them.

About nine o'clock Coach Snyder decided to have breakfast. He stopped at a roadside diner. The others parked behind him.

Snyder and the white boys went inside. Jesse and his black teammates stayed in their car. They could see Snyder talking to a woman behind the counter. She was shaking her head, no. They knew that meant Negroes could not eat at this diner.

A few minutes later, two of the boys came outside with plates of fried eggs and stacks of sliced bread. The food was passed to the black athletes. They had just started eating when they heard a loud, angry voice outside the car.

"So *this* is why you wanted extra food," a man snarled. He was a big fellow with a white apron tied around him. The boys guessed that he owned the diner.

"You got paid, didn't you, mister?" one of them said.

"I don't want money to feed any *niggers*," the man shouted. Then he reached through one of the car windows and began grabbing the plates of food. Silverware went flying, and the fried eggs spilled on the floor.

He carried his plates back to the diner. The hungry athletes had to eat what food was left, from the floor.

That afternoon Jesse ran as hard and as fast as he ever had. He had to win that day, and he did. But winning didn't make him feel any better. He was still burning with rage inside.

Later that year he was sent to the Olympic Games. These games are held in a different country every four years. In 1936 they took place in Berlin, Germany.

Athletes from all over the world were there. The best of them would win medals to take back home.

Jesse entered four events. The first was the broad jump. Many other jumpers were also in it. But the one man Jesse worried most about beating was Lutz Long of Germany.

People had been telling Jesse that Long was very good. Soon he would see for himself that it was true.

Each jumper had to qualify, to prove that he

was good enough to be in an Olympic event. And he had only three jumps to do it.

Lutz Long jumped so far, when he qualified, that he set a new Olympic record!

When it was Jesse's turn, he ran slowly at first and then picked up speed. Soon he was running as fast as he could.

At the takeoff board that lay in the ground, he leaped in the air with all his strength. He was sure he was jumping farther than anyone.

But before his feet hit the ground, he heard someone call, "Foul!"

His jump wasn't even measured, because he hadn't jumped where he was supposed to. He had started his jump six inches beyond the takeoff board.

Now he decided to take it easy. He didn't want to foul again. He ran slower the second time, and he didn't jump so hard.

But the jump was no good. He hadn't gone far enough to qualify.

There was only one jump left. The huge crowd in the stadium waited quietly to see if he would make it.

Jesse was so nervous now that he had to walk in a little circle to keep his legs from shaking. He looked around. There was no one to help him. He was all alone.

He began to feel faint. He gasped for breath. If he fouled again, he wouldn't be in the broad-jump event. He *had* to make it, yet he was just too frightened to jump.

Suddenly a firm hand gripped his arm. Jesse Owens found himself looking into the clear blue eyes of the man who was his rival.

"Hello, I am Lutz Long," the man said.

"Something is wrong. You are a better jumper than this. You *must* qualify."

Jesse nodded his head, yes.

"Measure your steps again," said Long. "Take off six inches in front of the board, and jump as hard as you can. Don't be afraid. You won't foul."

Carefully Jesse measured his steps from the starting line to the takeoff board. He put a folded towel on the ground, so he would see exactly where to jump. Then he walked back to the starting line.

He began to run. He hit the spot beside the towel and shot into the air. When his jump was measured, he had qualified by more than a foot.

In the actual event Lutz Long's best jump was nearly twenty-six feet. He broke his own record and set another new Olympic mark.

But Jesse Owens beat him. Jesse's record jump was *more* than twenty-six feet.

After Lutz had tried and failed to beat the American, he ran back to shake Jesse's hand. Then he held Jesse's arm up in the air and shouted to the crowd, *"Jesse Owens! Jesse Owens!"*

A hundred thousand voices called back. The stadium rang with the sound of Jesse's name chanted over and over.

He won the highest award for the broad jump, a gold medal. Then he won two races and a relay. When the Olympic Games were over, he had four gold medals.

Jesse Owens had gone to Germany with only one suit of clothes and $7.40 in his pocket. When he left, his suit was wrinkled, and he didn't have a penny. But he was coming home a hero. His family could hardly wait to see him, but they were not the only ones.

Thousands of people stood along the streets, cheering, when he arrived in New York City. His

picture was in every newspaper. Parties were given to honor him. Everyone wanted to shake his hand and talk with him, but nobody offered him a job.

It wasn't easy for a black man to get ahead then, not even an Olympic hero.

Jesse went home to Cleveland. He wanted to finish his last year of college, but he needed a job first. It took him a long time to find one.

He went to work in a city playground. The job paid very little, not nearly enough to support his family while he went to school. Jesse and Ruth had one daughter then, and a second was on the way.

One night two men came to see him. They had a plan they said would help Jesse earn a lot of money.

They were starting two Negro baseball teams. The teams would travel around the country, playing each other. Jesse Owens would travel with them.

Jesse was interested. He thought he would like playing baseball. Or maybe he would take care of the teams as they traveled. But the men had a different idea.

They wanted to use Jesse to get more people to pay to see the teams play. Their idea was for him to run a race with a fast horse before every game.

Jesse said no. He would feel like an animal, doing such a thing.

"Think about it," said one of the men. "We'll be back."

Jesse thought of nothing else. The idea of racing against a horse made him sick. Still, if he earned enough money, he could go back to school. He thought and thought.

When the men returned, Jesse told them, "I've changed my mind. I've decided to do it."

Three times a week he raced against a horse, while crowds of people watched him. He was miserable. He felt worse than an animal. He felt like a slave.

He quit after a few months. He couldn't stand the job anymore. But he had enough money to finish college.

Before the school year ended, a man came to him and asked, "How would you like to make a million dollars without lifting a finger? All you have to do is lend your name."

The idea sounded too good to be true, but Jesse agreed to it. He signed some papers and became one of the partners in a new dry-cleaning business. Soon Jesse Owens Cleaning Stores were opening all over Cleveland, and in other towns, too.

Business was good. Jesse was earning more

money than he had ever seen. He bought a big house for Ruth, himself, and their children. There were three daughters now. He also bought a home for his parents.

One day he tried to reach his partners and found that they had all left town. Why? he wondered. Then he found out. They all owed a lot of money and had left him to pay it.

Jesse had not saved any money. So every cleaning store was closed, and all the equipment was sold. It took him five years to pay back what was owed. He had to sell both houses.

It made him sad to move his parents into a shabby little apartment. They were old now. He had wanted them to live in comfort.

In 1942 Jesse took his family to Detroit, Michigan. There he helped hire workers for the Ford Motor Company. The Second World War was on. A great many men were needed to build motors for trucks, tanks, and planes.

At night, after work, Jesse taught basketball and other sports to a group of boys. On weekends he gave speeches at club meetings. People paid to hear him talk about the Olympic Games.

Soon he realized that what he enjoyed most, of everything he had ever done, was working with young people.

In 1949 he and the family moved to Chicago, Illinois. Jesse went to work for the state. His job was to help boys who got into trouble with the police. He knew they needed things to do to keep them out of trouble. So he organized baseball and basketball teams, and he trained the boys to play quite well.

In 1955 the United States Government sent Jesse on a good-will trip around the world. He talked to schoolchildren and young athletes. They always made him tell about winning his Olympic medals. He was called the Ambassador of Sports.

Back in Chicago he went on the radio. He played recordings of Negro jazz. He also traveled more and more, and spoke to schools and clubs.

Many times Jesse Owens has gone back and forth across the United States and to other places in the world. He talks about the Olympic Games, and he also talks about something he has believed in since he was a boy growing up: brotherhood.

Jesse believes that all men are born equal, no matter what their religion is or their color. Not everyone feels as he does, but he wants them to, very much. That is why he travels and talks to so many people.

He remembers how his parents struggled to bring up their children. He remembers eating fried eggs off the floor of a car back in Indiana. He knows things are better for some black people now. He hopes things will get still better. He also hopes it will be soon.

Jesse Owens died in 1980

ABOUT THE AUTHOR

Mervyn Kaufman's first Crowell Biography was the well-received *Fiorello La Guardia*. About Jesse Owens, Mr. Kaufman writes: "His life is as much a story of sorrow as of triumph. His success was not only in winning four Gold Medals at the 1936 Berlin Olympics; it was also his surviving—and dealing with—the bitter aftermath."

Born in Southern California, Mervyn Kaufman attended UCLA and then came to New York City to study journalism at Columbia University. He has edited and written numerous books and articles for both children and adults. He lives in New York City with his wife, Nancy, and their daughter, Amy.

ABOUT THE ARTIST

"When you think of Jesse Owens you think of motion," says Larry Johnson, who has conveyed the same feeling in his lively, exciting pictures. As a black sports illustrator, Mr. Owens found this assignment, his first picture book, especially enjoyable.

Larry Johnson was born in Boston, Massachusetts, where he first studied art at Canton High School and later at the Museum School of Fine Arts. As sports illustrator for the *Boston Globe,* Mr. Johnson lives in Roxbury with his wife, Valerie, and their two children, Nicole and Larry, Jr.